R B K
A REKINDLED LOVE

PART 1

MY LIFE MY STORY MY JOURNEY & A TALL TALE

Copyright © 2nd Edition 2024 R.B.K.

All rights reserved.

No portion of this book may be reproduced in any form without written permission from the publisher or author, except as permitted by U.S. copyright law.

CONTENTS

AUTHOR BIOGRPHY	V
INTRODUCTION	VII
AN R B K READ	
1. ONE INCARNATION NUMBER ?	1
2. TWO DARK NIGHT OF THE SOUL	6
3. THREE REBIRTH:	10
4. FOUR SYNCHRONICITY:	21
5. FIVE THE HEART BUBBLE	24
6. SIX TWIN FLAMES	32
7. SEVEN SEPARATION:LETTING GO	36

8.	EIGHT DREAMS	41
9.	NINE SPIRIT GUIDES	44
10.	TEN ENDING 2019	47
11.	ELEVEN THE 3-D WORLD	52
12.	TWELVE 20 - TWENTY	57
13.	AN EXCERPT	59
14.	ONE SPRING EQUINOX 20/20	60
15.	TWO MIDNIGHT	70
16.	GLOSSARY	72
Fullpage image		75
Fullpage image		76

AUTHOR BIOGRPHY

First-time author and poet. Canadian-born RBK is from northern Alberta. A tradesman and custom motorcycle builder who is one of the most down-to-earth people one could ever meet. Solitude is his closest friend, which allows him to ponder man's insanity. And if you asked him. **What was life like before insanity?** He would answer. **You tell me!** Continuing to experience his spiritual awakening he shares his journey. And what he has learnt along the way. Father of two and three granddaughters. He continues to ride with the wind at his back. Confronting daily the biggest challenge of his life. To search out and find his authentic self. Some may consider him insane. **But insane he is not!** Just a humbled man with an extraordinary story to tell.

THE PAN

AN R B K READ

INTRODUCTION
AN R B K READ

What you are about to read chronicles one man's journey out of the darkness and his ascension toward the light. All the lows and highs, ups and downs, on his roller coaster ride. That he endured to fulfill his mission and find his purpose.

At the time I started writing this book, I had come to a fork in the road and decided to take the path less travelled. And follow my soul to wherever it would lead me. My heart also played a major role. Leading me every step of the way. And delivered these words to each and every page through my fingertips. Always knowing that I had found home in an unexpected way.

I was asleep and lost within the illusion for most of my life! There are no words to express the gratitude I feel. For without Theresa. This book would have not been written. This book is for HER.

SONG REFERENCES ARE GIVEN WITHIN THESE PAGES THAT FOLLOW MY STORY HAVE A LISTEN IF YOU LIKE

ONE
INCARNATION NUMBER ?

READ*ON

I remember waking up between 5 am and 5:15 am for about two weeks. I never thought anything of it at first. But then it became too frequent not to question. As the days passed I felt different in a way. That I could not explain to myself logically. But my heart knew all along and eventually let me in on the secret.

I was nobody special just a man living in a programmed society. Trying to live in a 3-D world of greed and materialism. Always knew deep down inside that there was so much more to life. Then what I was taught by my teachers and parents. And then at age 59. I crossed paths with a wonderful woman who turned my world and life literally upside down.

1960 was the year. March 22 to be exact. This was the day that my new incarnation was to begin. Born into a working-class family where my mother stayed home and raised my brother and me. While my father chased the dollar night and day. Like so many in society do.

My childhood for the most part was pretty much normal. Just another kid being programmed by teachers and society without even knowing it. Education of course was part of the 3-D world. That prepared the students for society. Everything they needed - so they would be like everyone else. And enter the world with the belief that if they followed the criteria laid before them all would be fine.

At this point in my life, I graduated from high school. I knew deep down that this adventure that was called adulthood. Was going to be quite a ride and maybe even an illusion.

As I entered the workforce, I tried different areas of work that were available. Trying to find my way and get a foothold in our society. But still had a hard time finding a place where I fit in. While in high school, I had no idea what I was going to do for a living. So was left to just wing it and see where I would end up. While moving from job to job. There was always the rumour that the trades were the place to be. Good money for eight hours a day. And if you were lucky you could join a union. With all kinds of benefits. With abundant work at that time. So, I decided to explore the pipe trades. Went to trade school got some trade tickets under my belt. And ventured into the world of plumbers, pipefitters, welders and every aspect of the pipe trades. Times were great in my life my programming was in sync with the world. But in my gut, something told me to look at the bigger pitcher!

As I travelled through life year by year. Guided by my generic programming to be like everyone else. I stayed true to it all. Found someone to share my life with. Raised two children, bought a house and settled in for the long haul. Focusing on making money to purchase material items. It was great, this is what everyone did. But once again something told me to look at the bigger pitcher!

The years came and went and suddenly I found myself looking for work more often. Life became more of a challenge and within this challenge. I found myself alone. What had happened? I was following my programming just like everyone else and bang a complete detour. At this time. I decided to delete the programming that had taken me this far. And forged ahead letting my heart lead. Yet again something told me to look at the bigger pitcher!

The bigger pitcher was always there now in the back of my mind. Just there simmering and always challenging me to dimensional thought. This time in my life I was content with solitude. Inciting deep thought whenever I wanted. Finding people to converse with on a deep level is quite hard to find. And lucky for me I have some soul mates who can relate to subconscious thought. And I do thank them for that.

I learned to live a life of solitude along with adding in a bit of social activities. While twisting the wick on custom Harleys built in my garage. **THIS IS WHAT HAS KEPT ME SANE FOR YEARS.** Building something from the ground up is very satisfying. Riding down the road knowing that it is all you that put this bike in motion. But something was still missing in my life. And just could not put my finger on it. I had all I needed. Wonderful children in my life, some money in my pocket, a shack to live in, food in the cupboards, and Harleys to ride. And yet still could not figure out what was missing.

My new life of solitude, building and riding Harleys continued. Along with live music and using some 70's analog equipment in my basement also kept me sane.

I had always been spiritual and knew that the whole universe was connected in one way or another. For quite a few years I attended church services every week. Had my children baptized etc. And after all the weekly rituals. Began to question the dogmas of religion. That created parables from the four periods of history. Influenced by Roman religious dogmatic teaching became confusing. Dispelling all spirituality. So I strayed and went to search elsewhere.

My search led me to Sylvia Brown a world-renowned psychic. After reading many of her books. Opened my eyes to many things. Which resonated with me deep in my soul. So, as I continued with my new solitary life along with subconscious thought. I continued to build and ride Harleys and expanded my insight. Not at all concerned about what the programmed of society thought. About living in the 3-D world. The world to me was entirely different now!

Different in a way, that I perceived everything to be not what it seemed to be. But what it was. On a deep level, my soul understood. This of course could not be explained to anyone but no one needed to know anyway. I was once again content with my life. The solitude with deep thought confirmed. That I was finding some of the answers I was searching for. That had eluded me for years. Answers and analysis from deep thought that resonated with my soul pushed me further. To a point where I decided to eliminate and restructure my life materially and spiritually.

The material changes that I was making were mostly due to the fact. That work was getting hard to find at times. Also supporting myself was just getting too expensive. I wanted to be able to ride which kept me sane, so I made changes.

While searching for work I continued to ride and explore deep thought. A lot of times sitting in graveyards which gave me some solace. From the chaotic world in which I lived. Life was yet again changing. Once again something told me to look at the bigger pitcher.

At this time in my life, I began to spiral down into the depths of my soul. My soul was crying for help. I foraged for needed answers. But clarification seemed so far away. That I became disillusioned with life itself and entered the dark night.

READ*ON

TWO

DARK NIGHT OF THE SOUL

THE DARK NIGHT

Let's trip back to the 16th century, Saint John Of The Cross a Spanish mock coined the term "DARK NIGHT OF THE SOUL" in one of his poems (Noche Oscuia). This is the beginning of a spiritual journey that plunges the attendee into a spiritual depression. One begins to feel lost, hopeless and consumed with melancholy. Loneliness and isolation begin to set in and one feels that life is meaningless. Desolation, disconnection and emptiness. Totally separate one from the divine.

Questions are asked what is my purpose? Why am I alive? What is truth? A new mind-set is sought after regarding life. Being betrayed or forsaken is also questioned.

As I entered the dark night. I also entered my fifth decade of this incarnation and it was turning out to be quite a ride. Full of lows and highs ups and downs a roller coaster ride which I wanted to exit. Everything about the night was held within myself as I led my life of solitude. After all not many would understand unless they went through it themselves. This dark night which had taken me by surprise. And not quite knowing how to proceed. Decided to spend the spring summer and fall riding and socializing. Letting my free spirit take the throttle. I let the v twin rumble in my ears riding at will. Spending hours riding contemplating life and trying to fit the pieces together. As I was accustomed to deep thought my puzzle began to take shape but it was a large one! The puzzle was coming together as I emerged from the dark night.

 With the **dark night of the soul** behind me. I forged on. It seemed as if it was never going to end. Thankfully it did. My life came back on track and it was full steam ahead. With one outcome from the night. My awareness seemed to have sharpened.

 The economy was in full swing now and there were some bigger projects happening around the city. I was able to land a couple of jobs which would take me to the end of October 2016. Had a good run and saved some money.

 Now that I was at another crossroads so to speak. I made the decision to work in my shop at home through the winter. And ride once again in the spring of 2017 through to the fall. All was great throughout the year but as 2018 crept in I felt the strangeness again. Knowing instantly that the **dark night** had returned. Different than previously. I knew on a soul level that this second wave of the **dark night** reappeared for a specific reason. And my heart let me in on the secret much later.

 In 2018 I worked a bit here and there. In my shop at home while living with the **dark night.** Keeping myself mostly isolated from society as best I could. Riding of course. Taking in live music at some of the venues around town. Kept me sane as 2019 was ushered in.

 As 2019 rolled in like a tsunami. The **dark night** catapulted me to the darkest place. That I have ever been in my life. The hopelessness and loneliness along with the isolation. Made me withdraw from myself to scrutinize new perception regarding life.

The desolation, disconnection and emptiness along with being totally separated from the divine made me disillusioned. And I started to analyze real purpose.

The economy was standing still. My many years of experience and age. Was not opening any employment doors. Thy world was crumbling around me. With a solution needed ASAP. I did have some savings for retirement **is there any such thing?** But using it would only send me two steps backwards. Option number 2 may be some part-time work! Just something to bide some time until the economy picked back up. Job hunting we go.

Looking for work these days has changed a lot due to the computer. All you need to do is find it. The **dark night** had me bogged down and it was challenging to get motivated each day.

Job fairs were something new. For me anyway. Big box store – plumbing retail. I landed a minimum-wage job with a 120-day contract part-time. Well great! I can keep the lights on!

In January 2019 somewhere mid month. I was awakened from a dream that was so vivid. It startled me. Not really a nightmare. More of what I would call a dream message. The dream revealed that I had died and was sewn in a bag in which I was trying to escape. The vision haunted me for a time but a strong sense of intuition. Told me that a message would manifest when appropriate.

My new job in retail was scheduled to start the last week in March/2019. Was a little bit nervous of course but just rode straight into the new adventure.

Still in the clutches of the **dark night.** I forged straight through day and night. And continued where I had left off with the puzzle. More pieces fitting together more easily than before. This second wave of the night seemed to have shed more light on the puzzle. Therefore enabled me to distinguish between society and the bigger pitcher. Going through this second wave of the **dark night.** Heightened my thought process and allowed me to visit the grey area of consciousness. Where man hides his lunacy.

After going through the **dark night of the soul twice** the second being the worst for me. I am thankful for what I have learned and the insights I gained about the bigger pitcher.

THE DARK NIGHT

READ ON

THREE
REBIRTH:

NEW*BEGININGS

The last week in March was approaching quickly. And the dark night was still lingering in my soul but I persevered. The bigger pitcher became even more clear coming out of the dark for the second time. That I confronted my retail job head-on. New people and a totally different way of earning a living were all new. Those that I met were welcoming. The first four days were spent getting acquainted with the job through computer programs of information.

My work schedule was all over the place being that I was only part-time and on contract. But I needed to keep the lights on. Plus on the other hand, had time to ride and work in the shop. So, it was a win-win.

By the end of my first week. My computer-generated work schedule was ready. My hours ranged anywhere from 7 am to 10 pm seven days a week. This was the criteria for hire. Making it hard to get used to. And I remember looking back. I was pissed in a way. But understood that the greed of business influences control over the working-class man.

The next week I found myself working on the floor serving and helping customers. Which I did enjoy and began to develop a knack for the job. Being in the trades made me quite efficient. And along with my years as a tradesman. Could educate customers on the right and wrong ways of doing things.

As the week progressed. I was introduced to fellow employees by my coworkers in the plumbing department. By the end of the week, I had met a few more coworkers on my own. And was starting to settle in and enjoy the nonchalant atmosphere of the retail world.

Two weeks into the job. All had gone well. Working among customers from all walks of life. Made me realize that people are more concerned about the material world than the bigger pitcher. In the evenings when it would be a bit slow. I did have some time to interact with some customers. But found it was hard to find anyone whose vibration was similar.

As week three commenced. I was settled right in. And had become familiar with the way management operated. And should I dare say? They sure could have used some help! But it did not matter. I was there to keep the lights on.

The plumbing and paint sections were right across from each other with the aisles lined up. So I was able to see all the paint department from the plumbing. One day I noticed someone working in the adjacent department that I had not seen before. Never thought anything of it finished my shift and headed home.

My next shift was an opening shift at 7 am. So needless to say it was very slow for the first hour. While I was preparing for the day with another co-worker from the plumbing department. I was introduced to Theresa from the paint department.

Right at that moment of meeting her, I felt her vibration and knew that we would be friends. From that point on we would converse with each other. When we had the chance while working. And through small talk learned that we were different but the same. As we continued our friendship. I started to be drawn to her in a way that was strange to me. Unfamiliar but familiar. This caught me off guard because this scenario was utterly different. Than anything that I had experienced before with other people.

Every day I felt myself emerging from the dark night and began to feel more like myself again. With new insights of course. My new friend seemed to have awakened me from a dream. I was full of energy and could not wait to get to work when the schedule called.

One thing that I did enjoy about my new retail job was the music. Having collected music all my life. Listening while on the job was all right with me. Music is the water of life it can cleanse, clean and heal you. From the effects of the world around you. Music has been a salvation so to speak. For me throughout my life.

Now everyone has their personal preference. But I am a straight-up rock and roll, blues and country rock sort of guy. It is the lyrics that catch my ear every time. That pulls me into the personal aspect of the song. Some thing about the lyrics written in the seventies and sixties are mind-blowing. Furthermore can touch you on so many levels.

As I have mentioned lyrics always catch my ear and while working one day. I had heard a song phrase. **HOLDING ON TO YESTERDAY.** Now being busy with customers interferes with being able to listen attentively. So I pulled out the flip phone and accessed the notepad.

Finishing my shift I headed home. Searched YouTube and low and behold a song by Ambrosia recorded in 1975. Now song phrases are used by the ancestral beings to send messages. To souls who are climbing the ascension ladder. They are part of synchronicities used to communicate and will be discussed in a chapter to follow. `I keep holding on to yesterday - I keep thinking that I'm lonely - but it's only missing you inside - lord I don't know when I'll see you.` These song phrases resonated deep down in my soul. And filled my heart with a longing for home. Another Ambrosia song that resonated with me was. **YOU'RE THE ONLY WOMAN** affected me the same way.

Atlanta Rhythm Section **SO INTO YOU.** With song phrases like. `I am so into you - I can't think of nothing else.` Literally stopped me dead in my tracks. **IMAGINARY LOVER** by ARS same effect. As time passed by and the job continued. I just rolled with the music and every time these certain songs played. They seemed to relax me with a sense of destination and arrival. And then one day while having coffee with my new friend. It all started to make sense.

Being that many of the employees were part-time. Coming in to work at different times of the day. Having coffee times line up was just about impossible. Except for this one fated day when it happened. My new friend and I just continued a conversation. That we had started earlier that day without skipping a beat. Just like we were old friends. I can see so clearly today as I write. A strand of her hair hung over her face to one side. Within that moment of time. I was reminiscent of the past that was familiar. As this did shed some light on the song phrases. Which had resonated with my soul especially **holding on to yesterday.**

Wow, this experience expelled the dark night that was lingering. Allowing more light to enter my soul. I was uplifted with a sigh of relief. I had discovered my way home.

I never felt uneasy around my new friend like some people make me feel. It was more of a magnetic attraction. With a warm feeling that at times. Would feel like butterflies in my stomach. Then simply disappearing to a feeling of home and contented bliss.

I could not wait to get to work each day that I was scheduled. Feeling so good to be in her presence. Able to converse and share life experiences with my newfound friend was overwhelming. The next morning I woke up with a strange feeling that this day would be different!

As I prepared for work. With the weird feeling still lingering abound. I commenced to head out the door. Opened the door to a beautiful sunny and warm day. Blue skies with a few clouds hanging around. Unlocked the garage and jumped on the cycle.

It was about a forty-minute cycle to the big box store. Where my retail job was located. I enjoyed every moment of it. For I had always received the most wonderful smile. Anyone has ever seen except for that day. With part-time work employee's schedules don't always jive. Being disappointed understood the feeling from the morning. I can still see that reminiscent smile every day.

Within time I got used to her absences relishing the time when she was at work. It was always about that sense of home. I felt while in her presence. Her kindness and energy. I was changing inside and Theresa was absolutely the reason. I would learn the reason after my 120-day contract was finished and left my retail job. Which was the hardest thing I have ever done.

Some might say that this was all just a crush, infatuation or even lust. Or just being older and lonely. I can tell the differences between all of these. Not any did apply. I chose a life of solitude many years before. Coming to the decision. That I would not chase the elusive love. I had vowed to never seek. Always keeping an arm's length away. From the evasive love. But Theresa had a way of drawing me near. Therefore did start to question why.

The summer continued riding the panhead and working part-time at the big box store. Each day running into the next. Continuing to work on my new friendship which made me feel blessed to have met her. As my 120-day contract. Moved closer to it's end.

I woke up once again with an uneasy feeling. Jumped on the cycle and headed to the store. I knew my friend would be there. By this time we were sharing our schedules with one another. During our conversation that morning she informed me that she was to have four days off. My heart hit the floor. I could feel the pulse of my heart through my veins. My sense of home faded instantly at that moment. I wished her well and replied, `catch you on the flip side.` Now this feeling of abrupt separation that was about to begin. Stirred up some emotions that simmered within me for four days.

I fired the pan and rode every chance I could when my schedule allowed. The pan was in fine form. Always in top running condition. Consistently searching for new pavement. Where the pan could show it's strength. And growl on some fresh new hard top. Running strong the v twin rumbled in my ears. With the thought of my new friend's return.

As the fourth day came into view. The fifth was just around the corner and the tension let up. I awoke the next day like a child on Christmas morning eager to open their presents.

Grabbed my lunch and opened the garage. Straddled the cycle blasted off to work. Made record time that day! There she was as I walked through the entrance with that smile. As we walked by each other she commented `Did you miss me`? replying `You know I did`! Just so casual like we had said these words to each other time after time.

What a great day I felt at home again. This world and the lives we lead are so strange at times we do ponder them. But I knew right then and there that I did follow my heart home again! Does make one realize that there is a bigger pitcher and we all should be open to it!

Time to mention my love for music once again. It has helped me through life so many times. As it has people all over the world. Working at the big box store with music in the background each day. Made me look back at my own life. And realized that change had happened since meeting Theresa. And was open to any and all change. In the future.

Cheap Trick. One of my favourite bands from back in the day. Still going strong I might say. Who has had a string of hits throughout the years. Would be playing at the local casino. My son and I would be attending the show. Of course. Everyone has heard the single **I WANT YOU TO WANT ME** which was overplayed on the radio for years. That being said this is a killer song live.

So, one day as this song happened to be playing. Theresa walked by on her way to coffee and commented `"I love this song"`! I replied `"It will be better live at the casino"`! She did an about-face scurried into my aura and replied `"I best get some tickets then"`.

I can recall she was so excited about the show. Which was to take place on August 10/2019 at the local casino. I was very aware that she would be accompanied by her karmic partner. Which was ok with me. After all, we were just coworkers. Or was the divine working in the light? And were Theresa and I. Something more than colleagues?

We had arranged to meet before the commencement of the show. My boy and I arrived at the venue. Found a table and acquired a couple of drinks. I never did take to alcohol that well. Having sustained for the most part. I was anxious and did not look forward to the introduction of the karmic partner.

Shortly after we sat down with our drinks Theresa arrived. She approached me with that smile and hugged me. I introduced her to my son. Apprehension was high as her karmic partner walked towards us with their drinks. Pleasantries were exchanged along with introductions. Then off they went to gamble a bit before the show.

She looked beautiful with her hair down. New brown boots had been bought to go along with a brown leather jacket. A vision that has remained within my mind's eye to this day. I could feel her energy from our hug throughout the evening. Breathlessly anticipating to see her again. The energy from this brief hug was just a smidgen compared to our next encounter. Which would happen after my contract had expired.

As my contract end began to draw near. I became increasingly restless. With an uneasy feeling of separation that overwhelmed me. The recollection of the four days apart resonated very deeply. As my mind's eye began to count the days. These last few weeks were full of melancholy. Dreading my last day. Finding solace in knowing from deep in my gut. That this was just the first step toward my journey home.

I soldiered on through. Being drawn even closer to my newest friend. Savouring each day as if it would be the last. I could feel her energy stronger with each passing day. Theresa had become a part of me in an unexplainable sense of home.

July 23/2019 was my scheduled last day and it had appeared way too soon! I saddled the cycle and headed toward my last day. Now where everyone is more concerned about the material of the world. Along with hoarding all the cash they can. They have forgotten the simple pleasures of friendship. Losing themselves along the way. And one should be open to finding their way back!

In a previous conversation with my friend. I asked if I could leave her a card in her locker. On my last day since she was to leave before me, she agreed. And on the fated day, I was ready.

I had stopped in at a dollar store one day after work. Purchased a card and travelled homeward. Placed it on the table until I was ready. This was a pivotal moment for me as I decided what to write within it. I decided to be calm, cool collected and not sentimental.

I started to write. **We are just two souls on different journeys whose paths have crossed.** Mentioned a favourite song I liked and four lines of a poem. <u>Drawn to her - for only a moment - time stood still - and she was gone.</u> Which has continued to evolve. I had two pocket angles that I had been packing around in my pocket for years. Both with inscriptions on the back. One with <u>hope</u> and the other <u>always with you.</u> Decided to enclose pocket angel <u>always with you.</u>

Right at this moment as I write. I can't help but think about the pocket angles I never lost. And then passed one on to my friend! And why did I choose **always with you**?

Placed the card in her locker. When I arrived at work and headed out on the floor. Throughout the day we seemed to be both melancholy but accepted the day for what it was. Watching the clock tick, tick, tick so ever slowly. I received a message through my headset. That Theresa was about to leave. My heart skipped a beat or maybe two. I then proceeded to meet her at the main entrance. Where we conversed and shared some memories of the summer, and how great it was working together. She had asked me to make sure to visit when I could. And keep in touch. Of course, I agreed.

In that moment time stood still. And everything was nonexistent to me as I watched her walk away. She turned back smiled and said **"I'll miss you"** - I replied, **"I'll miss you too"**. Watching her walk away. Continues to be an unbearable memory.

I returned to the floor to finish my shift not quite knowing what I felt. But the longing for home would soon return. End of my shift - cleaned out my locker unlocked the cycle and rode home. The longing for home becoming more intense.

Music has always awakened my emotions and appropriately close this chapter out with an Etta James cover. Recorded by Gov't Mule. <u>I'd rather go blind.</u>

*ARTIST*B.LEMAIRE*

> **WITH A SMILE OF KINDNESS MY HEART WAS OPENED ALLOWING THE THE TEARS TO FLOW**
>
> ~R.B.K.

FOUR
SYNCHRONICITY:

GUIDANCE&SIGNS

The angels, guides and ascended masters have a system. That is used to guide and send messages to those who have awakened. Via thoughts, words, feelings, and visions. Guiding the soul to fulfill it's ascension. Potential signs are everywhere – number sequences on license plates, numbers on clocks or anywhere there are numbers. Now this can get very tricky. And one must learn how to correctly determine which numbers are a sign. Since numbers are everywhere.

When it comes to number signs. Ask your team of angels, guides, and masters. For some signs. And a willingness to receive the signs is imperative. One must remember. Not to go looking for numbers just let them come to you. Numbers that just all of a sudden pop into view. Or catch the corner of your eye. Appear on the TV, clock, your phone etc. When you least expect it. This can take a while to master. But as time passes you will catch on.

Once you master the knack of the number system. Find yourself an angle number book to decipher the number meanings.

As we all progress in our awakenings. We become more aware of our guidance and signs. And our intuition sharpens. Other forms may be used. Like, dream messages and my favourite music phrases. I especially like musical phrases because they can be so precise and to the point.

Now at this time, I would like to mention. That the process of guidance and signs. Will be a little different for everyone. But the concept is the same. Remember to just let it happen don't try to force anything. It will all evolve in time.

Walking in nature is a good way to clean your aura. While grounding yourself to Mother Earth. Signs can also appear in nature. So always be present in the moment ready to receive. Asking for signs and guidance is always recommended when needing answers and insights.

As your signs manifest. Keep a record of them. With a few details about how they manifested and the date. A lot of times the messages these signs convey do not make sense. Until later as the puzzle unfolds within your journey.

Guidance and signs can also be sent right to your conscious thoughts. Just like turning on the light switch. Cogitation may just occur. Maybe delivering a song phrase random words or a number. As I write my story on these pages. This form of information exchange has been evolving quite rapidly for me. And has been guiding me every step of the way. I have never been alone while I type. Which pushes me forward day after day. It is my journey that I pursue. Finding my way home! And I thank my dearest friend from the bottom of my heart for hitting the light switch.

Dream messages simply put. Information that will arrive during a dream. This method can be hard to understand at times. And may be unclear due to the clarity of the dream. So, I would suggest that you use a dream journal. To document the dreams. And hang a dream catcher over your bed. If you are having lots of dreams.

Ask your angels to help you remember them and to be vivid. Colour is always great! Journal everything you can remember about them. Date them and use them for future reference. After studying a dream. It is amazing what information comes to light days after. When evaluating the information you have received.

Keeping your aura clean while living in this 3D paradigm. Can be quite a challenge. With all the negative energy floating around. Meditation will keep your aura clean. And the more time you spend meditating the better.

Using meditation practices to help open your third eye. Will greatly help you to receive guidance from the Angelic realms. Along with meditations for all seven of your chakras and kundalini. Is a must. To activate your kundalini and keep your chakras in line.

Once you have embarked on your journey. You will start to ask questions and seek answers. There will be no turning back! You must delete everything in your life that serves you no purpose. Let go of the 3-D world. Begin to unfetter all that holds you there. Embrace the 5-D world of Aquarius and humanity's evolving consciousness.

As I write my story on these pages. This form of information exchange has been evolving quite rapidly. Guiding me every step of the way. I have never been abandoned while I type. Impelling me forward each day and night. This is my pilgrimage to find my way home! And I thank my dearest friend Theresa. For her inspiration.

FOR "HER"

FIVE
THE HEART BUBBLE

FOR THERESA

SOULS
ADRIFT AND
LOST IN
TIME ALONE
SEARCHING
FOLLOWING
THE LIGHT
LOOKING
FOR HOME R.B.K.

It was late afternoon when I arrived home. From my last day of work at the big box store. Feeling out of place and numb. Fired the pan and went for a rip. The rumble in my ears sounded wonderful. But did not hide the sense of separation that reminded me of the past. I backed off the throttle. Let the pan relax a little and headed home. Cranked up some Skynyrd and settled in for the evening. Thinking about the invitation to visit.

Now I would like to reiterate this was not a crush, infatuation or lust. Furthermore, this was not about some old burnt-out biker who was lonely. I was content with my solitude and was not looking for anything. My life had been propelled into the unknown. Where more questions had to be asked and answers found. It was the absolute feeling of home which followed me everywhere. That needed to be answered. I slid into bed that night worn out from the ride late in the day. Falling asleep thinking of where to look first.

The internet what a great tool. It does bring the world closer together. But one needs to remember that every Tom Dick and Harry using it. Is not reputable in the information they distribute. So, discernment and caution are needed.

My search led me to a site called Quora. Which was a question-and-answer social media site. Wow, I had ventured into this ridiculous realm! Needing some time to focus. This website gave me the chance to enter into some deep thought and evaluate my journey. Knowing that it may take some time to find some truthful answers.

The world of the internet is an immense void that one can get lost in. Having kept myself from being pulled in. I began to seek and search. As I continued to surf the Quora site. I stumbled upon a website called Loner Wolf. Which introduced me to all kinds of information and the phenomenon of twin flames. Which I had never heard of before. That was intriguing. So I read on.

From that day forward. I was hooked on the information available on this site. Absorbing all that I could take in. Furthermore, two of the editors of the site were twin flames. Having experienced many of the topics. Written about on their website. Great this made everything a bit more credible. Feeling that I was going in the right direction. As I searched for answers and clarification. With discernment of course.

I was learning so much. I realized that there were people all over the world living in similar scenarios. I was not alone.

As the days past the longing for home increased. My world became small and dark. I had thought that the dark night had reappeared. But no, it was something much more different.

While I adjusted to being unemployed the yearning for Theresa intensified. All that I could do was focus on my friend. Who would creep into my mind whenever she wanted. I could feel her energy constantly and contemplated the thought of a visit. I continued to keep my act together. Keeping to myself, riding the pan, keeping up with the yard work etc. And one day decided to visit.

Friday August 9/2019. The day before the Cheap Trick concert. Jumped on the cycle and peddled north. As I got closer to the big box store. I became very relaxed. Walked through the sliding doors. No Theresa in sight, she was having coffee. As I turned and walked into the lunchroom. Our eyes locked on each other. As we threw our arms around one another. Time stood still. The energy intense. I was home once again.

The brief reunion lasted about fifteen minutes. Said our goodbyes and confirmed that we would see each other at the trick concert.

I exited the sliding doors and unlocked my cycle. Riding away from the retail store. Still reeling from the intense energy exchange. The longing for home grew. As I rode further away from her. Having been invited back again. Gave me some peace. As I write these pages. Sometimes I consider my sanity. But I felt the path was true!

Not long after our bittersweet reunion. I started to have some changes in my sleep patterns. I was being awakened between 5 am and 5:15 for about two weeks. Looking back. On all the information that I was absorbing from the Loner Wolf site among others. **I would like to remind everyone to follow your heart when searching for information on the web. Because of all the misinformation out there.** I became aware that this was a sign from the Angelic realms. That my spiritual awakening had started and to pay attention.

The spiritual awakening and ascension process. Are both different for everyone in a variety of ways. Everyone must follow their fated path.

As time passed. Personally, my world started to worsen. I became swallowed up with emotions of separation and a deep sense of homelessness. Always reflecting on the memory of the four-day separation. But these intervals of more than four days between visits were unbearable at times. The only cure was another visit and I was always welcome. The next encounter with my friend. Would explain and bury any doubts that I may have had regarding my journey.

I was very relaxed as I peddled the cycle toward the retail outlet. Home grew closer with every rotation of the pedals. Entering the sliding doors once again. I approached Theresa with total ease. It was all perfect. Home yet again.

As we commenced into conversation. I found myself lost in her eyes. Both of us seemed to have lost track of time. Only the two of us within that moment. As we awakened from this state. Our eyes met to the connection. Nothing was spoken. We both felt that same moment. Seeing it in her eyes. At that instant, I knew without a doubt that she was my home. And more visits would be needed to keep me sane. So I hoped.

Arriving back home. Knowing that I had already incorporated one more piece of the puzzle. Moved me further forward in my journey. And or pilgrimage. Now cognizant of where my home was. I saddled the pan and went for a rip!

With all the information that I was imbibing. The puzzle of my journey was starting to piece together. With one questionable piece. Where were these familiar feelings from? Why do they subside when in Theresa's presence? I would expand my search for answers.

More answers where would I look? I asked myself. The internet and some websites were fueling my quest. However, I needed deeper insights pertaining to my journey. Now that we have entered the age of Aquarius. Psychics have entered the mainstream of the spiritual community. Helping people while using their gifts. Now to find a reputable one! After searching for a while. I found a person whom I could trust.

Psychics have all kinds of abilities. And each psychic may have only one or many of them. Including clairvoyance, clairaudience, clairsentience, claircognizance, precognition or even empathic abilities. Aura reading, channelling and scrying are some other abilities that can be used.

I had some questions that I thought would move me forward. Asking if I should pursue a friendship with my co-worker. Strong energies were sensed between the two of us. I was on the right path. And what I desired with her would be manifested. In the proper time for the highest good. Now I was moving forward with some definition of my plight.

Another question came to mind. With reluctance, I asked. Have I met my twin flame? Yes, you have. And a new beginning is on the horizon. Well, the puzzle pieces were fitting together. Parts of my journey were starting to make more sense. The intensity of Theresa's energy grew even stronger with the answer to this question. But the longing for home remained.

Before I continue. While on your journey don't forget to take notes of everything pertinent. As you look back the puzzle pieces will fit more easily. You will begin to see the journey unfolding. Right before your eyes. This will give you better direction.

Third question. What would be the age of my soul? A very mature old soul with deep spiritual awareness. Extreme wisdom with a free spirit. On his last incarnation in the 3-D realm. I was also informed that my new friend had an old soul as well. I liked this information source and decided to schedule a five-card tarot reading.

The day had finally arrived. I was excited about the tarot card reading which was about to happen. First card drawn. NEW BEGINNINGS CARD. This was the first step toward a new beginning and new adventure. Step into the unknown and create positive life changes. Inner change was happening within. And was to proceed with wise thoughtful care. While facing inner belief with courage. Looking forward to a more positive relationship in the future alongside my TF. This new beginnings card was the second time it had been drawn. Once previous to this reading.

Card number two. THE SHADOW CARD. Represents sensitivity and emotions. Nothing in life stands still. Being called to action the time is now. Fears will need to be faced. As you look into the dark shadows of your soul. Confront what has been avoided and courageously walk through. You and life will naturally balance. With light at the end of the tunnel. No longer denying the past. Let the tears fall. This cleaning process will wash away and clear out anything hidden and pushed away.

Another card that resonated with pertinence. These first two cards explained so much. Had seemed to guide me forward. I was relieved and continued my quest. Gathering information collected from the Loner Wolf site and following a reputable YouTube channel. With caution, I may add. I blazed ahead one step at a time. Always knowing my path was true.

Third draw. STRENGTHENING BONDS CARD. The potential exists for greater stability within the relationship. With yourself and your TF. Be realistic about what you can expect and offer in return. Be constant and clear in your actions and demand the same. Use the down-to-earth approach. Expectations are likely to be met and the relationship strengthened. Ground yourself steady and calm. The energy will secure a strong relationship.

The fourth card drawn. MANIFEST CARD. A time of great power for you - anything is possible. All the tools are at your disposal. To create anything you desire. Love unconditionally, support, cherish, listen, understand, forgive, be kind joyful and even silly. Use these tools and work your magic. When you come from a place of love. You will generate love. Be honest in your intent and manifest your heart's desire. You can achieve anything you put your mind to.

DREAMS COMING TRUE. Contentment wishes fulfilled. Card number five. Entering a time of peace, joy and satisfaction. Be clear about what you want. In a relationship to look like. Wishes may be granted soon. Be open to receiving all that the universe is sending your way. Express gratitude when dreams come true. Feeling good sit back and enjoy. Partake in activities that give you pleasure. This will aid in your wishes being fulfilled and manifested.

These were all great cards. As I read them carefully a few times began to realize. They were drawn in a sequence that detailed my journey card by card. As I re-read and edited this page. I became distinctly aware of this. Just as a thought entered my mind! Like switching on the light. WOW!

The longing for home by this time had invaded my aura. And was part of my everyday life. With me, 24/7 always knowing where my home was. A forty-minute bike ride north. My perception of my life of solitude was beginning to change. Feeling a hunger deep in my soul. Time for a visit was approaching.

I had scheduled some windows and doors to be installed in my home. And required some door hardware. This would enable me to visit. Passing on a couple of Sylvia Brown books. For Theresa to read. Since she was interested. As I entered the lumber department walking toward her smile. Our eyes met one another locking for an instant. Time was then lost in that moment once again. Within our conversation, I had mentioned that since meeting her. My life had changed. She replied, "IN A BAD WAY". Answering I replied. "NO! IN A GOOD WAY OF COURSE".

I had always felt at ease when around her energy. Finding that the visits were helping me after a separation period away. While in separation her presence was always there. I could not hide from her. She was there whenever she wanted to be. Night or day. Day or night.

As I settled into unemployment. Late summer had begun and fall could be felt in the air. Working on the pan, yard work, and housework kept me busy. Along with riding the pan to keep me sane. But could not shake her presence and energy. Which was felt constantly. Along with the feeling of home on the horizon. I decided to follow my gut feeling. And research the twin flame phenomenon more thoroughly.

Twin Flames had been mentioned in my tarot card reading. With the new beginnings card. Confirmation that I had met my twin. Was received and clarified. So, I ventured to find answers to complete more of the puzzle. I recall meeting my friend from the paint department. Thinking our paths did cross for a reason.

FOR HER

SIX
TWIN FLAMES

With the dawn of Aquarius. Numerous people are being awakened to 5th-dimensional energies. Repressing their egos and leaving the 3-D world behind. Walking toward the light and finding the way home. Finding their purpose and freeing themselves from the negativity of the third paradigm. While balancing their masculine and feminine energies.

As souls in the 3-D world. We are all learning lessons along the way. Evolving with each incarnation. Lifetime after lifetime. Reincarnation was introduced to me through the books of Sylvia Brown. I had always believed and never questioned it. It was just a given. Something that resonated in my soul to be true. Advancing our souls. Is one part of our mission. To achieve a spiritual awakening when the time is right. And begin our ascension with divine guidance.

One must complete six soul stages while advancing toward a spiritual awakening. Infant soul - Baby soul - Young soul - Mature soul - Old soul - Elder soul. Now these soul definitions will vary from one source to another. But you get the drift.

Now I have mentioned the **DARK NIGHT OF THE SOUL.** In this incarnation. I have had two of them. At different times prior to my awakening. These dark nights. Were not the catalyst for my awakening. Like it can be. Mine was different. One that would install three pieces of my puzzle. As souls progress on their journey. Advancing each incarnation. While ascending spiritually. They start to feel the need for unconditional love. And start to seek this out in the 3-D paradigm.

Look at the 3-D world in which we live. One cannot dismiss the fact that unconditional love does not exist. In the 3-D Earth matrix. Just look at the world! Unconditional love only exists in the 5-D paradigm. And the Angelics have a plan. The plan has always been in play. But since we entered the age of Aquarius it has sped up. The 5-D paradigm is on its way. As more and more people wake up. Ascending spiritually and consciously. Unconditional love will flourish. Heaven on Earth will become a reality. This is where the **TWIN FLAME** phenomenon enters the pitcher.

After each incarnation, we head home. Of course, we do travel light. Nothing is needed from the third dimension. Once arriving at home again. We settle in and organize our next incarnation. The whole trip everything from. The lessons to be learnt, our birthday, birth parents, relationships, education, jobs etc. I mean every aspect of the incarnation along with free will. Everything is documented recorded and written down. The incarnation contract signed. All are stored in the hall of records. At the time of conception, we are launched into our next incarnation. Here we go again!

All souls do not have a twin! Twin Flames are very rare souls. From other planets and star systems. Once twin souls join in the physical 3-D world. They become twin flames. Together their joint mission will begin. Jointly they share the same soul energy propelling them to further. Their divine mission of spreading the message of unconditional love to the masses. Twin flames are the salvation of the world. That has been orchestrated by the divine. They have signed a contract to fulfill their mission. In the rapture of the Aquarian age.

Some twin souls enter into a contract which involves incarnating within the same century. This will enable them to seek each other out. Awaken and go through the process of ascension and transformation. Each follows their individual path and timeline. Until the time is right for union. Divine guidance will play a pivotal role in the timing of union. Once they find each other their soul energies merge. They become twin flames and the mission is initiated.

The twin flame journey is not an easy task. It is riddled with riddles, twists and turns, ups and downs. Lows and highs a roller coaster ride. Which one never forgets. The twins must first purge themselves of all past life traumatic experiences. Cut all karmic cords. Cancel any contracts past present and future. Complete any lessons to be learnt in this incarnation. Rid themselves of any karmic vows and debits. Balance their feminine and masculine energies to a fifty-fifty balance. Practice self-love. <u>**Very important!**</u> Meditate daily to keep their chakras aligned and balanced. Also, keep their auras clean. Free from the negativity that surrounds us daily in the 3-D world. Awaken their kundalini. This is no easy task twin flame or not. But rest assured everyone has a team which includes. Angles, Guides and Ascended Masters who are with you every step of the way. All this spiritual work that one must accomplish. On their spiritual awakening ascension will raise their vibrational frequencies.

Twin Flames will need to overcome other difficulties. That they may encounter on their journey. Obstacles like large age gaps and religious differences. Distances apart from one another, different races, marriages to karmic partners. And any other social dogma that is deemed unacceptable in the 3rd dimension. The large age gap is very spurned within society. But twin flame couples are the same age. These obstacles can cause confusion. Therefore not accepting the connection felt. Run from it. We must remember at this point their souls know the connection. However, the 3-D awareness of the matrix twin does not. Also, one of the twins is awakened spiritually more than the other. Therefore commences toward a friendship or relationship. While the matrix twin runs away. Known as the chaser and runner phase. This goes back and forth between the two. So the couple have a chance to experience both phases. There is also a separation phase. Which gives them time to work on themselves and the ascension process. Preparing for their union. Each TF couple's journey is unique. With different obstacles to confront and tackle head-on individually and together. Sharing their unconditional love with the world. In the hope that the world will see and live by their example.

Twin souls that do not incarnate at the same time in the same century. Will not be able to connect with their other half on the Earth plane. But will be able to in higher dimensions. For those souls who have been incarnated at the same time in the same century. Having agreed to find each other. Signed their soul contract. Will find each other with divine guidance.

Wanting to embark on a twin flame journey. Is not something you wake up to one morning. And decide you are going to do. It is divinely orchestrated and has been preplanned according to an incarnation contract. Which has been signed by the participant. You can not go searching for a twin flame journey. It will find you! If you are a twin soul!

I would like to end this chapter with the remembrance of a song from 1969. **LONE ME A DIME.** Boz Scaggs recorded this timeless tune. Along with the late great Dwayne Allman and other remarkable musicians. Surfing YouTube one early morning. I stumbled across a live recording from a Scaggs concert in 2010. I was so moved by this song. Tears rolled down my cheeks and reminded me of the home I had found. A forty-minute cycle ride north.

As my research into the twin flame phenomenon ended. I assessed the gathered information and pondered it. What have I learnt? Were any of my questions answered? And were any of the puzzle pieces fitting together? Yes, questions were answered. As the puzzle continued to piece together. I had learnt a great deal about the connection of twin flames. Explaining to me why the feeling of home followed me everywhere.

SEVEN
SEPARATION:LETTING GO

Sitting here in front of my computer. Contemplating how to start this chapter. I reflect on the past. Revisiting moments of times past. With a smile upon my face. The faint whisper of a tear is heard. As it hits the floor. I remember how my life was turned upside down. And was catapulted into the eye of a hurricane. Without knowing the outcome. Later to realize that fait placed me there.

As fall approached and the air began to dry. The pan was calling. Fall is my favourite time to ride. Harvest time along with colored leaves falling. The cooler days making way for winter. Theresa's energy was felt every day. As my visits were growing longer apart. I began to feel a need for change from within. Flay my skin so to speak.

I started to look at myself and discard all that needed to go. Personality traits I no longer valued. Addictive behaviors. Any of the seven deadly sins that I had acquired. An old diet. Watching the news and reading the papers. Was pushed aside to the never again section. Long-time friends disappeared. A thirst for the spiritual increased. I felt the load lighten. But Theresa was there whenever she wanted. Night and day.

Meditation has a long history. Dating back thousands of years. It keeps your chakras in line and balanced. Protects your aura from Earthly negativity. Helping with the uncoiling of your kundalini. And opens your third eye. As my odyssey unfolded. I added meditation to my daily routine. Working on my chakras, kundalini and aura. I could feel her energy increase. As my routine continued. Whilst my unstable emotions.

During this time of my journey. My emotions were overwhelming. Something that I was not familiar with. I had always been an emotional person. But this was a different feeling. It was as if my heart exploded and the emotions burst through my eyes like raindrops. Letting go of trauma that my soul had endured for numerous incarnations. Eventually, I was able to balance my emotions with some divine help. <u>**FEMININE AND MASCULINE ENERGIES NEED TO BE AT A 50/50 BALANCE AS WE ENTER THE AGE OF AQUARIUS.**</u> I learned to live with that constant feeling of home. Reminiscent of it's origin. And channelled the energy into <u>**MY LIFE MY STORY MY JOURNEY.**</u>

Taking a short break before I continue at the keypad. A feeling of calm passes over me. As it lingers for an instant. Realizing that the person who has inspired this book. Is only a fifteen-minute bus ride away. Quicker on the pan!

I persevered with my search. As my journey continued to unfold. More of the puzzle came together. Her energy and the longing for home still resided within. While I am able to balance my emotions now. They are still felt but controlled. And the phenomenon is ever so real.

Twin souls mirror one another after their energies have merged. And recognize each other on a soul level. At this point, the mission has been initiated. Unknown at this time to both. The awakening process has begun. Awarenesses start to surface. One soul will be more receptive than the other. Hence the runner and chaser phase mentioned earlier.

This was the catalyst that propelled me inward to look at myself. The summer spent with my friend Theresa. For those 120 days.

Looking at my reflection in her eyes. Inspired me and gave me the strength and courage needed. To change and create my authentic self. This was a step closer toward the light. But still as faint as the lighthouse from the open sea.

With the commencing days. The lighted lighthouse became brighter and brighter. Sunshine was replacing the storm clouds. And the rumble of the v-twin kept me sane once again. The longing for home and her energy remained. Never leaving me stranded alone. As late fall approached

Collecting music and taking in live music has always been important to me. Throughout the years. Keeping me sane much like the pan. Living in this 3rd dimension. Can take its toll on all of us occasionally. Therefore, live music has been a refuge for me.

The mirroring effect that had led me to look inward at myself. Was lengthening my time between visits. My gut feeling and intuition told me to keep working on myself. To raise my vibration. Time for the next visit would manifest when ready. Though Theresa's energy was always pulling at me constantly. If I let my guard down. I would seem like a stalker to the 3-D society. If visits were too frequent. And separation is good for all twin flames.

Loverboy was to perform at the casino on November 1/2019. I had not been to a concert since Elton John in September. I was excited they always come through. It had not snowed yet and the crispness in the air was inviting the dread of winter.

A soul mate of mine rang the bell. We headed to the casino. Where I had previously attended the Cheap Trick concert. We started our conversation where the last one had ended. I was content in the moment. Taking with me the energy of home along for the ride. Never straying far from the memory of the Cheap Trick show.

Arriving early. We decided to grab a drink in the lounge. And hang out until the show started. Conversations are always uplifting with a soul mate. That you have spent many incarnations with. The time passed by quickly. We headed to the show. Entered the venue. Located our seats which were near the front. Eighth row back. Off to the side. Right in line of some decibels. Just what I liked. Bring on the show.

Now preshow there is always music playing until the act hits the stage. A collage of music to entertain. As I listened a variety of music was heard from the 60's 70's etc. When low and behold *I WANT YOU TO WANT ME* was being played. I tripped back to a moment in time at the retail store. Recollecting my co-worker's response *I LOVE THIS SONG.*

Messages and guidance are sent from your Angelic team in many ways and forms. This song being played. Meant to me that I was on the right path. And to continue with my journey. As you spiritually ascend you will become accustomed to messages of guidance. Learning how to decipher them will become easier.

I am learning to let go and not fight the process. Let the Divine guide me. Flow with the stream. Let go of the 3-D paradigm as much as possible. Recreate a newer version of myself. Balance my feminine and masculine energies, continue to meditate and raise my vibration.

While working on the above. I continue the search for my life's purpose. Concluding that writing this book has been part of it. A divine plan is unfolding. As the puzzle grows larger with each piece installed. I am evolving. Processing new information. Focusing on the light ahead of me. Travelling into the unknown. Following my soul in the direction of home. Knowing that my journey commenced at the convergence of two paths. Where home was inadvertently found. Both paths leading the direction home.

There will always be a battle between the logical mind and the heart. That one must learn to control. Follow your heart, your intuition, your gut. The logical mind functions in the 3-D world and analyses from the Earth plain. Willfully directing you in the wrong direction. There will always be a tug of war. But in the end, the heart wins every time. When you are tuned in to it.

You may have noticed that while writing. I wonder off-topic from time to time. Diverting from the main storyline. I have found that I can add a bit of my character to my story. After all, it is my story. That started at the juncture of two paths. And with my character traits added within the words of this book. Hopefully, they make me out to be more real than not.

This wondering has tripped me back to my last day of work. When a Paul Davis song flashed through my mind. I GO CRAZY. After all, maybe there is a love story written amid these pages?

I awoke one morning. The sun pierced through the curtains right toward my eyes. I could feel the heat through the glass window. Relaxing for a bit longer. I gathered my thoughts and decided to visit the retail store. I needed some milk crates to store some records in for a future move.

Being that it was November the weather was cool. Along with ice and snow. So decided to take the bus there and walk home. As I entered the building searching. I could see Theresa was very busy. And headed off to gather my storage items. On my way out we exchanged smiles as our eyes met. Home again! Time stood still for an instant. Her familiar energy. The kindness within her smile. Nothing needed to be said. She knew why I was there. Her smile confirmed our connection. At this point in my journey, all doubt was extinguished. My heart and intuition confirmed the phenomenon is real. Logic was nowhere to be found!

I would like to clarify at this time. That one twin of the couple. Is always more receptive and awakened than the other. This being the awakened counterpart. Both knowing the connection on a soul level.

That was my last visit November 21/2019. Christmas was advancing quickly. With not much holiday spirit within. Realizing that the twelve days would be different than any twelve before. I prepared. Not knowing what to expect.

Reclining. Waiting for a cup of tea to cool a wee bit. Pausing with an exhale of purpose. Understanding that all I need is on its way. While my mind flashes back to 1981. ELO'S TICKET TO THE MOON. Reminding me of HER as I turn the page.

EIGHT
DREAMS

The Dark Night of The Soul can be the catalyst for a spiritual awakening. Each person is different. For me having two dark nights. The first awakened my soul. And the second prepared me for the catalyst to come. Near the end of it. Embarking me on my ascent upward. Dreams can also prepare the soul for its awakening.

Dream messages. What I like to call them. Can be hard to interpret. They can be foggy. Like there is a mist in front of your eyes. They may be in black and white or colour. With or without sound. Still images or movies. All in all. Dream interpretation takes some work and practice.

First, hang a dream catcher above your bed. Use meditations to help open your third eye. And ask your team of angles, guides and masters. To help you interpret your dreams more clearly. Remembering them once you awake. Also, keep a dream journal. Recording all your dreams. Until you start to notice any that reoccur. Take note of the recurring ones first. They will show you guidance to follow and choices to make. Of course, this scenario will play out differently for everyone in different ways.

I am trying to strengthen my ability in this area. By using meditations to open my own third eye. The meditations are helping this to improve. Dreams are becoming more vivid with sound and colour. I hope to use the dreams to gather information concerning my future. And have had some breakthroughs. During a recent dream. I consciously heard the number 43. Instantly woke up and wrote the number down. Before returning to sleep.

As I awakened the digit had not been forgotten. 43 was written down. Climbed the stairs to the main floor. Made myself a cup of green tea. Glancing through the pitcher window. A snowstorm was stirring outside. Nice and toasty in my shack. Food in the fridge good day to write.

Hit enter. Logged in. Accessed the Kindle reader. Opened the Angle number book. Found #43. <u>**Angels and ascended masters are with you - supporting and loving you - mentally talk to them about your hopes, dreams, fears - ask them for help - they will always come to your aid when invoked.**</u> Always knowing that someone has your back each day is a great feeling.

As I entered my fifth decade. I was a blind man in the dark. Until Fait joined me at the junction of two paths. Where I met another traveller. Heading in the same direction but using the opposite path. As we headed east on different paths. Speaking softly as she started off <u>**"I'll see you soon."**</u> Disappearing under the lighted moon.

Meditation has many forms and uses. They have been used for centuries. In all kinds of cultures. Prior to my awakening. I was aware of the skill but never practiced it. Since then, I have realized the importance of the study. Encouraging everyone to meditate daily.

Meditating will keep your aura clean. Align and balance your chakras. Relax you after a day of third-dimensional negativity. Reenergizing your aura for the next day. Meditation has a long list of benefits for the soul. These are just a few.

Within the words written on these pages. I have mentioned some information more than once. For it's importance. To further pursue it. Adapting it within your journey toward the light.

Ending, I once again revisit the juncture where fait leads me. Like a blind man in the dark. An appropriate tune to close out this chapter. **WHEN A BLIND MAN CRIES.** Deep Purple.

As I continue to travel forward new information appears and I chase after it! Read on my fellow traveller.

NINE
SPIRIT GUIDES

This book mentions angels, spirit guides and ascended masters. Which we all have a team of. Watching over us 24/7. I would like to share a story. Apart from this one. About a spirit guide which I have been introduced to. So to speak.

I have always been a spiritual person. Knowing deep within that the astral realms existed and everything else that came with it. No doubts whatsoever. The parameters of time and space. Connect all parallel universes and dimensions together. But are also separate. I am just living in the 3rd dimension. But have been able to glimpse other dimensions. From time to time. Past, present or future through dreams and Deja vu. My soul travels from incarnation to incarnation playing a different character every time. Evolving and learning each time. Until the awakening process.

My father died Feb. 1/2011. A parent's passing can be a hard process to go through. After all, we do pick our parents for specific learning experiences every incarnation. My dad was born in the thirties. Grew up on a farm where he learned that hard work was a given. My grandparents from Poland. New hardship and immigrated to Canada after World War 1. My grandfather was a short man with a tattoo of a bull on his chest. Survived the first world war and taught my father how to survive in the 3rd dimension. Which was passed down to my brother and I.

Growing up I resented my dad. For his parenting tactics. Feeling isolated from the world at times. Growing older I realized the life lessons he had taught me. Acknowledging that he did the best he could.

People grieve in different ways. For when one passes we grieve for ourselves. Cognizing that life has not ended can be a great comfort. Understanding incarnation will help shorten the grieving process.

As the days passed, I became more receptive to the fact that Dad was gone. It was not the end of the trail. He had just travelled on.

Spirits, ghosts, apparitions, visitants or presence. Whatever you like to call them. They are very real to me and have been visited several times throughout my life.

Early one morning before dawn. I was startled awake by a strange feeling that I was being watched. While rising at the waist and turning my head to the left. Noticed a silhouette. Which had no intention of leaving too quickly. Not being shaken within it's presence. Gazed upon the visitor in wonder. Never did have a visitant stay so long.

A thin man close to six feet tall. Long white beard comparable to that of a wizard. Long and thick. Gleaming with a radiant white light. With a glint of silver that illuminated him completely. Dressed in a white robe. Tied at the waist with a cord of hemp. Using a crook to lean against. Simply gazing upon me and suddenly vanishing. Was this my departed father? Paying a visit. I never gave it a second thought until a physics reading a few years later.

It was explained to me while attending the reading. That I was accompanied through a tunnel of light. By a long-bearded person. Some sort of rebirth had taken place. And that this spirit guide has been shepherding me for quite some time. Never giving it much thought. Then remembered the visitor years before. More of the puzzle just fit together. What an astonishing divulgence. This did shed some light. On the new beginnings card.

Another revelation that came to mind. Shortly after the reading was an explanation right in sync with it. Every now and again my bed would literally. Shake at different times in the early mornings. Now needless to say this was a little alarming but did not terrify me. And would just ask them to go away. Since the reading, I have extended an open invitation to my quest. Assessing the information from the reading. And the bed being shaken. I understood that my quest was another spirit guide. Alerting me to be cautious and aware that day.

Now that I had established the link between the spirit guide and the bed. Needed some confirmation. One night as I slid into bed. Casually asked if he would shake the bed. A few moments later he did. Being able to interact with your team members is essential. They are always available. Mentioning again everyone's journey is different.

With every breath I inhale my soul expands. With every step, I take closer to the light. My heart heals. And my soul spreads it's wings and begins to fly. Searching for two intersecting paths. Where under the light of the moon. Home travelled east not so long ago. Whispering within her breath <u>"I'll see you soon"</u>. Disappearing under a starlit sky.

Exiting this chapter. I exit with yet another tune. <u>All for You.</u> Recorded by Cold Chisel. A song phrase that entered my thoughts and woke me one early morning. Dedicated to the inspiration of this book.

FOR THERESA

TEN
ENDING 2019

As November ends. December slumbers in with a whisper. Reminding me of the past year. Dragging with it a sense of melancholy. Followed by complete utter accomplishment. Reflecting back on my journey thus far. And with a sigh I continued to write. While the presence of Theresa's energy. Merged with my aura. Confirming her presence.

December brought with it the season of materialism. Along with loneliness for some. Stress for others and a multitude of emotions. Followed by overeating and headaches throughout the twelve days. All forgetting the reason for it afterwards.

With the start of December, I continued to write every day. Within my life of riley schedule. Not too concerned about work. Sharing my story is of immense importance to me. If I could just help others by telling my story. That would make up for all those wasted years spent. Emulating societal programming.

Turning down a couple of Christmas dinner invitations. Was hard but decided to go it alone. Cook myself some favourites and write. Christmas presents were already distributed and delivered. Cabbage rolls, ham and perogies were all ready to go with all the trimmings. Christmas solitude no stress, perfect.

Speaking of solitude. One of God's greatest gifts. That more people should embrace with open arms. And I don't mean a few days alone. In order to perceive solitude. And understand what it does to the soul takes some time. Looking inward at yourself. To discover who you really are. Letting your soul reveal all the bad and the good. Humans unconsciously entomb all the bad from their past and present. Burying it all within. Until their awakening after which it is all purged.

As Christmas approached. I had three visits from soul mates. Who have been following me around this incarnation. For some time. All perceive me to be eccentric and maybe from the dark side of the moon. But they are old enough souls. To comprehend and acknowledge that being divergent is good for the soul.

Soul searching is part of everyone's life at some point or another. But takes real effort and a conscious awareness of societal programming. Which I believe is an early stage of our spiritual awakening. Living in a programmed society. Where everyone is a generic template of one another. Needs to be acknowledged.

Seven days until Christmas. Having purchased some holiday favourites from the farmers market. Poppy seed cake, fresh vegetables, pickled garlic and homemade jam. Perogies were a must. Potato and dill.

Walking home under a warm sun. Not a cloud in sight. Having acquired all my favourites for the season. Smiled at the thought of my retail job and all that had transpired. Remembering Theresa's smile and kindness. Releasing a tear to fall amongst the fresh fallen snow. Anticipating her reaction to the book.

As I settled in for the Christmas week. I wrote, listened to music, wrote, worked out, ate, and wrote some more. Every day her engulfing energy propelled me to write. Meditation was now a tremendous help. At keeping my head clear. Which allowed the words to flow. Being guided every step of the way the book continued to evolve. Page by page one at a time. Day by day number by number. Have I found my purpose?

It has been nine months. Looking back can not believe the changes that have taken place in my life. Some drastic some still evolving. While others are transforming slowly. Two souls converged at two paths unknowing their fate. Separated at the juncture. My path leading me here. Recalling her whisper. I'LL SEE YOU SOON.

Looking in the mirror commencing some shadow work to start my day. Notice a grey beard emerging. Or is it white? Decided to let it grow. Shaving at the book's completion.

Shadowwork is basically looking at yourself in the mirror. Exploring your inner darkness and demons. Which will be part of your unconscious mind. These will be repressed feelings, ideas, perversions, guilt etc. Anything that darkens your soul will be entombed and hidden away. You must own 100 percent of your shadow self. Do not avoid it or repress it. To experience healing. One must confront them head-on.

Standing in front of a mirror. Gaze straight into your eyes. Examine who you really are. Concentrate on your inner self. Accepting what you find. Acknowledge it - own it - release it. Letting go of all that serves you no purpose. Practice this every day. To free your soul to soar. Write down everything that you release. Burning the paper afterwards. Rewriting them down should they reappear. Keeping them in check. Remember you do have free will.

The arrival of Christmas Eve. Disappeared quickly. Not really noticing. Writing had occupied most of my day. Cooking my favourites was under control. Making sustenance available whenever the need should present itself.

As the twelve days proceeded. The words flowed through my fingertips. Theresa's energy had grown so strong and constant. That our soul signature had unified. Sporadically feeling as though Theresa was controlling my fingertips. With ease and grace. I accepted it all.

With persistence, I wrote and typed. Being awakened after centuries of incarnations can be agonizing. Tormented with torment.

Not for the lighthearted by any means. There is no turning back once the ascension has started. You must confront and accept the challenge placed in front of you. Of course, you could just stop dead in your tracks and languish within your ascension. But what good would that do?

After my ascension started. I had to investigate the TF phenomenon. I was intrigued and fascinated at the same time. Always knowing that there was more than what the world would avow to. Confronted my fears and sailed into an unknown realm. Knowing all along that my soul was in the crow's nest.

My brief introduction into the astral realms years before. Would establish a starting point. Where I was able to start my puzzle and gather information for the book. I had perceived it all firsthand not letting the ink dry. Putting it to paper forthwith. Nearing the end of December. Twenty-twenty was on the horizon. New Year's Eve had crossed my mind. Finishing the book was imperative!

December thirty-first. Had not made any plains. New Year's Eve was yet another part of our programming. That I deleted years back. But the thought of spending it with someone. Would be embraced with open arms. It would have been nice to check out some live music. However, continuing the book was imperative. I wrote. Planning to attend the fireworks early that evening.

I had written most of the day. Later relaxing to an enjoyable meal of leftovers. With the lingering thought of a chance meeting with my friend. Expecting a great show lasting about twenty minutes. I kicked back with a cup of tea with anticipation. Lingering in her present energy as the show approached.

The evening was pleasant enough. Above 0 degrees Fahrenheit with a sight wind. Warmly dressed I departed. Noticing the sky as I walked. Stars visible among see-through clouds reminded me of a painting. A Starry Night painted by Vincent Van Gogh. A candle-lit village among the snow-covered mountains in the French Alps. Nestled under a starry sky. A beacon for any soul searching for a home.

As I drew closer. I could hear the boom and whistle of the show. Red, blue, green, and yellow. All colours that the eye can perceive. Weaving my way through the crowd I found a view. Taking in the show and closing out 2019. Sending forth a wish for the year to come.

With the crowd dispersing. I vacated and headed home. Not knowing what to expect in the coming year. Walking homeward under the starry sky. I wondered if my wish had been heard. Focusing my gaze upon the sky. Reflecting on the Van Gogh painting. The beacon had let me north toward my home.

Continuing home recollecting the previous year with a smile. Slid the key in and opened the door. Prepared some green tea and settled in for a viewing of <u>A STAR IS BORN</u> 2018. Followed by two Steppenwolf classics. <u>JUST FOR TONIGHT</u> and <u>ANOTHER'S LIFETIME.</u> Played loud of course. Twenty-nineteen was in the rearview.

FOR "T"

ELEVEN
THE 3-D WORLD

After your awakening. Living in this 3rd dimension can at times be a little arduous. You must discern and cognize. That there are many souls still asleep. Navigating through your day can drain you physically and mentally. Being exposed to negative energy. Will require meditation on a continual basis. As it is everywhere. Maneuvering through the minefield of sleepwalkers. Will send you searching for self-recognition. While asking yourself many questions.

As I exited the **dark night of the soul**. For the second time. A fair amount of my questions had been answered. The dark night. Had taught me to look deeper and not superficially. In this time of questioning. Remember your astral team is there to help you twenty-four-seven. Once again follow your heart. Your soul knows where it is going. Follow it!

The information road. Is a minefield riddled with misleading and informative information. Everyone's journey is different. No one can authenticate the information brought forward. The discernment will be your own. Recurring information should be followed.

Spirituality and religion are two separate entities. Spirituality exists in all of us. It is our own to use as we like. Religion is a form of dogma created by man. The ascension process is all spiritual. Led by your soul's spiritual awakening and soul growth.

The ego is a sense of self which is an illusion. Used as an evolutionary survival mechanism. Needs to be controlled. Quieted and eliminated as your awakening progresses. A spiritual ego can develop. Separate from the self ego. Your spirituality should be used to eradicate the ego. Not help it flourish.

Now that we have entered. The age of Aquarius. Human society is changing in unseen ways. Our DNA is changing from six strands to twelve. This has been proven in the scientific community. And is believed there will be a major DNA shift. In the near future. The DNA upgrade is part of the ascension process after awakening. Since we are all light beings. Having our DNA upgraded. Will allow more light. To enter our light bodies. Helping us to connect to our higher selves more easily. As the age of Aquarius commences.

This of course will take some time for a couple of reasons. First, the ascension process can take some time. Due to incarnation cleansing etc. Second, some people sometimes get stuck in the ascension process. While others may not be receptive. Needing a push. They will shift or be shifted. At some point.

Another big change that will start to surface and evolve is unconditional love. As the 5-D realm begins to replace the old 3-D paradigm. I've got your attention now! Many believe that unconditional love exists in the 3rd dimension. However, humanity has added compromise to what is referred to as unconditional love. Adding conditions to love. Inhibits the unconditional aspect of love itself. Compromise is conditional!

This is where the phenomenon of twin flames enters the arena. Twin flames are the salvation of the world. They will bestow upon the Earth unconditional love. That will blanket the entire world. By virtue of their love. Setting in motion harmony and peace for eternity. Heaven on Earth!

Twin flames have signed up for a very difficult task. Living within the third dimension. Manifesting full union with their beloved. They hold the key to unconditional love. That has eluded man for centuries.

As the new age is propelled forward. With unconditional love as its cornerstone. Governments will begin to transform. Followed by a complete reconstruction. Tyrants will stumble and fall. The greed will be extinguished. Corporation control will cease. World borders will be eradicated. Nuclear weapons abolished. The hungry will be fed! The fighting children within the sandbox. Will no longer govern the world. Human injustices will abate. The dawning of a new age will commence.

A new outlook concerning the planet's future. Will take precedence on the world stage. Healing will take place using cutting-edge technologies. Along with alternative energy sources. Repairing the planet from a hundred years of fossil fuel abuse. Generated and fueled by man's greed and his disrespect for nature.

As mankind further evolves and their souls receive more light. Their spiritual gifts will be perceived. New souls entering the world with twelve-strand DNA. Will have a newly designed template with 5-D abilities. These awakened souls. Will be the front runners of the old soul. And will carry no karma. Like their predecessors had.

Indigo and Crystal Children. Are a new group of souls returning for new incarnations. Their aura contains the colours blue and a deep purple associated with the third eye. The sixth chakra. Connected to the highest spiritual realms. They will be the bridge between humanity and spirit. Edgar Cayce (1877-1945) the sleeping prophet had predicted the arrival of these souls. **THESE SOULS CAN BE SEEN IN THE NEWER GENERATIONS.**

They will work in conjunction. With all the awakened of the world. Twin flames, star seeds and light workers. All here to heal and change the world in which we live. Everyone healing and changing the world in specific areas. Another shift in the evolution of man has already begun.

Every day my advancement of ascension propels me further up the ladder. At the pinnacle, a locked lynch gate. Marking the mouth of a familiar path. Looking through the gate I catch a glimpse of a juncture. Harbouring a faint silhouette. Where is the gatekeeper?

As I continue to write I feel a deep sense of self. Someone new and different. A hidden entity emerges. Finding tranquillity and peace. As I resume my story.

Scrutinizing the sea of souls as I navigate through my days. I ask myself how many are awake? Will the awakenings increase? Can I help in some way? These questions cross my mind from time to time. Intuition tells me the silhouette would answer.

Deja Vu has guided me most of my life. Within the last year has been obvious. Whilst writing especially. My intuition is also more honed. Strengthening your gifts through meditation is requisite.

To Conclude. Don Henley's **TALKING TO THE MOON.** Have a listen!

FOR HER

READ ON

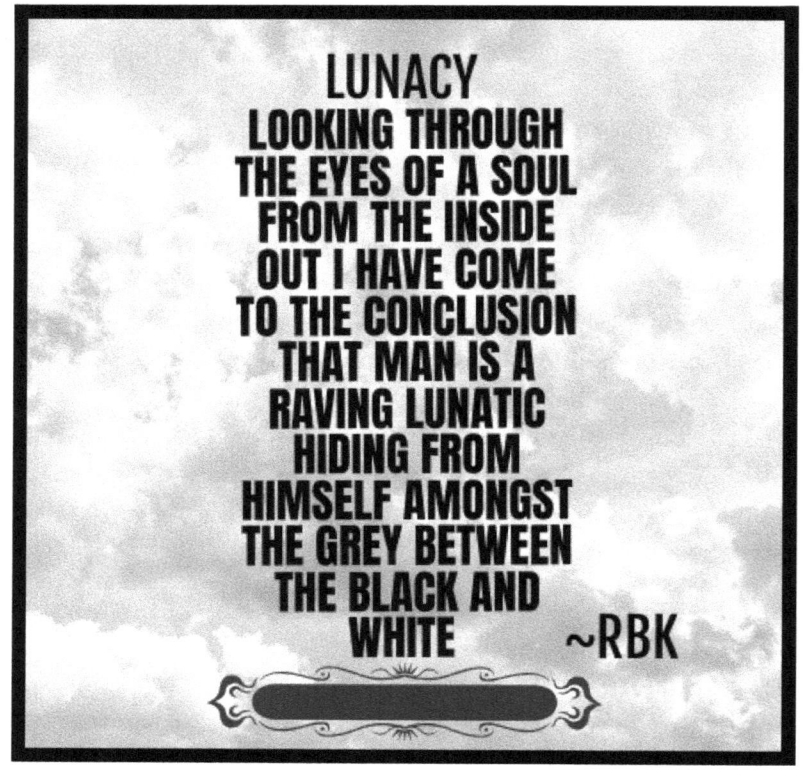

TWELVE

20 – TWENTY

Drifting off to sleep in the early morning of the first. Pondering if my wish had been heard. The Van Gogh painting danced in my dreams. Assuming the village candles would burn brightly guiding me home.

Employment opportunities seemed to have stopped. Pipe trades jobs vanished. Even the minimum-wage jobs were tough to acquire. Ageism is alive and well! I still had some cabbage under my mattress. So I decided to ride the winter out. Seeing what would transpire in the spring. Intuition told me to continue. I did and by mid-January. My book was nearing it's end. Excited about the prospect of my first manuscript and what would become of it.

At this point not being concerned about employment. I persevered and knew I would prevail. I was on the right path. Reminiscent of her words at the junction. <u>I'll see you soon.</u>

The winter so far had been quite mild. Just finished a week in the deep freeze. The weather had turned once again. Reminding me of spring and the rumble of the pan. I continued to type.

With the ink hitting the pages. <u>LOL.</u> I pondered would I find work? Or would I ride?

Follow my path, swim with the current, get it done, there is a plan. Mantras I would use every day to keep me focused on the result.

Among the falling snow spring was a distant rumour. As I pounded out the last chapter. Savouring the aroma and taste of a twenty-year Merlot aged to perfection. As the glass emptied two songs entered my space.

Gov't Mule recorded a tune written by Van Morison titled <u>**BALLERINA,**</u> Have a listen it is amazing!

White Snake wow! what a band! <u>**ALL I WANT - ALL I NEED.**</u>

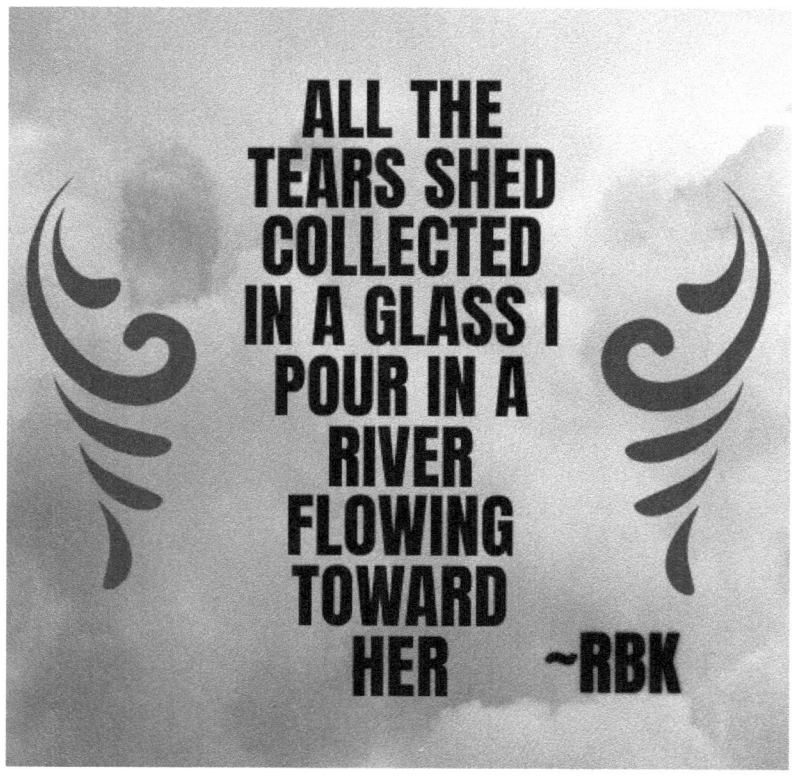

AN EXCERPT

Dear Reader,

On the following pages is an excerpt of two chapters. From the next of the Awakening Soul Series. MY LIFE MY STORY MY JOURNEY & A TALL TALE – KR & TALL book/part 2&3. My story continues within a story inspired by actual events and real people. I have included some of my dreams, a hint of the mystical and a wee dash of fantasy. Blending together a nonfiction read ahead of it's time. The book has been documented and written in real-time as my journey has unfolded. Continuing my story as the character KR. As I stepped into my new reality, where all things are possible.

With Love and gratitude.
R.B.K.

ONE
SPRING EQUINOX 20/20

A cold sweat had awakened him once again. The same vivid dream. Reaching for the Perrier under the bed. Gulped down some water. Laying back down KR drifts off to visit the sandman once again. Waking at sunrise recollecting the dream. While indulging in a cup of green tea. Poaching two eggs. Loading the toaster with whole wheat.

Standing in front of a locked lynch gate. Recognizing a familiar path leading toward a junction. The movement of a faint shadow was observed. The gatekeeper is nowhere to be found. The eggs were ready. Peanut butter jam toast. A large glass of milk. While ingesting the breakfast. Then chasing it down with the milk. Could not help but focus on the dream.

Rolling in around midnight from a three-day ride. KR was still tired. Decided to unwind and chill. Working on the chopper was always relaxing. The chain needed to be tightened. An oil change was due. It was that time of year when the v twin could be heard near and far. But KR could tell the difference between the old and new motors. He was old school. Simplicity was his motto. Preferring to build his own. Service and ride them. Having a reputation for simplicity and perfection in building. Pulling wrenches was his forte. There was always riding cabbage in his pocket. And a part-time job creating some extra.

Washing some clothes. While attending to some household choirs. KR grew tired and decided to have a siesta. Before working on the chop. The lazy boy would suffice. Sinking into his favourite chair. Drifted off to visit the sandman yet again. Once again visiting the lynch gate.

Stirred to consciousness from the sound of a shvl head motor. Smiled and exited the lazy boy. Opening the back door as the custom FXR rolled up the drive. The motor hot from being run hard needed a break. Not many used the shvl any longer. Production was stopped in 83. But anyone who did knew why. The RUB's not having a clue. Only interested in the stigma never understanding the culture. Were instant bikers weaned while watching Sons of Anarchy and American Chopper. Ramrod and KR were old school through and through. Societies stereo types riding Harleys before it was cool. Never paying any attention to anyone on two wheels wearing running shoes.

Ramrod hit the kill switch. Shutting down the shvl. A conjure of heat dissipated as it cooled. Sliding from the saddle stood and embraced KR. It had been a long while. Their conversation continued from where their last had ended. Innis & Gunn was always in the fridge. And KR offered Ramrod one.

There was a lot to catch up on. But the trivial would have to wait. More important topics would commence first. What was being ridden and built? And the second most important woman. Ramrod opened another Innis. KR had never been a big drinker. Eventually quitting the beer and indulging in wine. Now and again.

KR loved to create and building motorcycles was second nature to him. Living alone gave him the time needed to build. Having a new build ready to ride was important. While riding another. Another build in progress. Questions were answered. Ramrod had a build on the go, another Innis was opened.

The second topic was a little sensitive. Both learning to live with their fallacies. KR had kept women an arm's length away. For the longest time but recently not so much. Playing the field was what Ramrod did best. The trivial was conversed throughout the evening listening to music and breaking bread.

As daybreak crept through the curtains. KR could hear the shvl fire up. With a strong growl from custom-made straight pipes. The shvl was topped up with some oil. Ramrod suited up. Boots chaps leather jacket. Finally his beany and glasses.

With the clutch pulled in rolled down the drive. The pipes were warm. Releasing the clutch Ramrod headed south twisting the wick. The 103 cubic inch stroker thundered through the crisp spring air. Disappearing like lighting. It had been a memorable visit. And KR looked forward to the California trip. That was planned together that evening. The maintenance was still needed on the chopper. KR had plenty of time before his five-hour shift started. Working part-time at the retail outlet. Put more riding cabbage in his pocket. And of course, there was Theresa.

Slipping into a pair of older-than-new Denver Haynes. KR entered the tranquillity of his shop. The chop always received the TLC required and in return always came through. Growling on the hard top the pan always ran strong and was his favorite. Not many could understand his obsession with the old motors. He didn't care. The original four motors had been tried and tested. Simplicity was the key to a breakdown situation. Checking his pocket watch time to go. As he prepared for work. Glancing in the mirror. The reflection had changed. Not the facial features something else.

The new build consisted of a spaghetti frame manufactured in California by Atlas Frames. Heavy wall one-inch tube. Old school all the way. Hardtail of course. Thirty-eight-degree rake. Ten inches over in the down tubes. Six inches were added to the backbone. One inch more to the seat post. Spoked wheels. Duel disk four-piston callipers mounted to a twenty-one-inch front wheel. Sixteen-inch rear wheel and four-piston caliper. Five-speed transmission with taller gears. Motor to be run 103 cubic inch cone knuckle with extensive work! The date for the California trip would be scheduled at the next drop-by.

It ended up being a wonderful day. Not a cloud in sight 69 degrees. Recalling the visit from Ramrod. KR wrenched on the pan. Ready to rock for the next rip. A five-hour shift and the sight of Theresa would round out his day superbly. Theresa made KR feel at ease and enjoyed her company. Happily calling her his friend. His intuition apprised him of something mystical. One of those broads that just draws you in. The Inns & Gunn would need to be stocked up!

Warm evening with a slight breeze adding some crisp air. All the ingredients needed. KR suited up as the pan was warming. Strapped on his lid. Slid in the saddle pulled in the clutch loaded up first gear and headed west. Receiving an earshot of valve float. As the pan redlined between shifts. Asking for more at 110.

Backing off the throttle as a favored terminus entered his sight. Green grass cemetery. KR pulled in the clutch found neutral and coasted toward the gate. No gatekeeper. Opening the lynch gate recollecting his dream as he entered.

Tranquillity was always found there. Peacefulness was abundant. And time, endless. He had always found cemeteries alluring. The sun played peek-a-boo with the clouds. Periodically casting a ray of light toward the Earth. Warming the ground. KR found a place to sit and rest. Grounding himself with Mother Earth. Closed his eyes and visualized the enchanting smile he had received earlier that day. With a slight sigh smiled to himself.

As the sun set. The moon made its appearance. As the pan growled down the hard top. Heading toward the Tower & Crown. A local pub where the food was exceptional. The bangers and mash anyway! The pan came to rest in front of the main entrance. Pipes hot and the oil thin. Leaving his beany on the solo seat. KR entered and found his usual stool vacant. Ordered the mash and a classic. Knowing the day was about finished. Theresa was still very reminiscent in his thoughts.

No one ever bothered him. KR was the typical stereotype. That seemed to have travelled seven decades into the future. Carrying a 70-year-old pocket watch. However, utilizing motors not in production did attract attention. Only from interesting people.

Finishing his plate. He swallowed the remains of the classic. Paid his tab and vacated the pub. Ignited the pan for a warmup. Engaging a hot little number in conversation while waiting. Slid her his business card. Saddled his ride and idled toward the interstate. The brisk ride home was invigorating. Soon enough he arrived at his shack.

A sixty-year-old bi-level with a detached garage. Considered a shack by the yuppies. Only to be demolished and rebuilt. Bought and paid for dry and warm. KR called it home. And its door was always open.

Preparing for some shut-eye. KR warmed up the turn table. Gently placing a blues album on the platter. The blues do make the world feel so much more real. As side B finished sleep was needed.

Crawling under a feather tick that his grandmother. Handmade years ago. Made him feel tranquil. Climbing to the clouds he floated into slumber. Tossing and turning throughout the night. Found himself standing in front of the lynch gate. Once again locked. The gatekeeper is nowhere to be found. Peering through the gate just beyond the junction. He observed a rope bridge crossing a deep chasm. The bridge lighted throughout it's length. At the portal of the bridge a silhouette. Holding a lantern hanging from a crook. Beckoning him to approach.

Staring at his reflection. Trying to make sense of his dreams. KR put them on the back burner. And concentrated on the build. He would take advantage of his day off and create. The solitude was overdue!

A miserable day was waiting on the other side of the door. A sporadic drizzle with broken-up clouds and a cool 60 degrees. Sliding the key in the shop door. KR entered his. Own little heaven. Some machining was first on the list. The shop was a builder's dream. All the tools needed lathe and milling machine. Welder, drill press, oxy-acetylene. Tire machine hand tools etc. Collecting tools for the shop was ongoing. Throughout the day KR was focused on the task at hand. Concentrating on the build. While savouring a cup of Earl Grey. A reflection of Theresa appeared behind his eyes. Taken back by the vision. Continued to savor the tea envisioning a midnight rendezvous. Stepping outside for a clean breath of air. The sun was making an appearance. The pan would roll and thunder later.

The build was progressing. The tins were ready for paint. Black of course. And the oil tank for powder coat. Over the years the shop had been stocked. Parts were always on hand. For regular maintenance.

Finishing up his day in the shop he headed in for supper. The slow cooker was busy all day. Working its magic on a blade steak. Baby carrots and onion were also included in the mix. Along with a potato. A side of corn would round out the meal. Ending with a cool glass of milk chased by another. What a pleasure it would be to break bread. With his new friend, he thought. Waiting for his tea to cool.

With a belly full of grub. The pan-warming KR suited up for a rip. Still dialing in the new lock-up pressure plate. Installed earlier in the season. Was anxious to test a new setting. Straddled the pan slid in the saddle released the clutch and headed west.

Merging onto Gibbins Ray Drive. He could feel the pressure plate doing its job. With a slight grin, KR twisted the wick. Letting the valves float between shifts. The drive train hooking up better than ever. Further testing would need to be done. Affirming some new blacktop could be found.

Glancing in his rearview mirror. A newer model gaining ground. Dropping from five to three was an easy feat for the pan. With a snickering growl, the red line jumped turning on the pan. Eighty ninety-a hundred still pulling. The rear view was empty. Backing out of the throttle making a left turn into Green Lily's Graveyard. A running shoe rider whizzed by. KR speaking under his breath. `"Sure could use some pipes"`! Having a fear of speed separates the experienced from the novice. Maintenance and awareness are key factors to survival.

Green Lily's was another favourite stop. As the sun started to set KR took a load off. Sitting back reflecting on his day as the sunset. Speculating on what tomorrow would usher in. Having been reminded that women could still stir his soul. One anyway! It was getting late time to head home.

Sunset ushered in the night. And with the added cloud cover dark was the night. KR hit the road. Backing out of the throttle was his motto at night. Abruptly exiting the shadows, a porcupine shit! Grabbing third gear leaning to the left gracefully piloted the pan. Around the obstacle. As the rear tire collected some quills. With his heart racing KR continued homeward.

Entering city limits he decided to stop at the Tower & Crown before heading home. A bowl of hot soup sounded good. Rolling in the pan came to rest. Removed his lid and slid from the saddle. Recognizing the hot little number from his previous visit. Introduced herself as he entered.

KR sat at a table this visit. Approaching his table. The tall blonde from outside. Shawna Lee just happened to be an employee. A large bowl of beef barley and a classic. Spinning around heading toward the kitchen strutting her stuff. Glancing back in his direction.

One bowl was not quite enough. A second was ordered. The thought of a beer was followed by a craving. Simply vanishing like lightning. Putting an end to his craving. It had been years and Inns was the only beer he would consume. The second bowl was up on deck. Delivered with a smile along with the tab. On his way out a spliff was offered. Turning it down. Started the pan. Headed home to his shack.

The moons waxing crescent lighting up the sky. Would make for an enjoyable ride. The pan was eager and still warm. Riding south KR found some fresh black top. Making a mental note for a future visit. As the cool wind tossed his ponytail from side to side. The smoothness of the v twin whispered a compelling question. **What** was life like before insanity? He had forgotten! But then again. Every man had his own answer! He would sleep in a bit and run some errands before his shift at work.

Viewing his reflection. Drew his awareness of the subtle changes occurring within his character. Subconsciously and consciously. He welcomed the change and felt new beginnings ahead. Deciding to walk to work would do him good. Clear his head so to speak.

Walking to work took him forty-five minutes. Crossing a footbridge along the way reawakened his dreams. Striding through the downtown core. Across another footbridge climbing a grassy kopje. Found himself at work. Pondering to ask Theresa out?

Six to ten pm was his scheduled shift. The walk had been invigorating. And contemplated walking some more. Considering the weather of course. Theresa had already left but would catch her on the flip side. He was apprehensive of the outcome. Stepping up to the plate was motto number three. But had a good feeling overall.

Arriving home around eleven. KR felt a shiver of the blues heading in his direction. Poured himself a goblet of merlot. As he watched the legs of the wine. Run down the inside of a long-stemmed goblet. Captain Fantastic and The Dirt Brown Cowboys serenaded him to sleep. Drifting into the world of dreams. He found himself yet again in front of the lynch gate. The falling goblet hitting the floor stirs him from sleep. Stumbling off to bed until sunrise.

Sunrise brought with it an early morning shift. Seven till noon. KR decided to walk once again. An early morning dew was melting as the crisp air warmed. He would use the same route. Keeping to the trails and out of traffic. Nearing the two-way crosswalk. A chance meeting with Theresa occurred. Thinking to himself how convenient.

Living in the surrounding neighbourhood. She would occasionally walk to work. KR was euphoric. What a great start to the day. Answering his question with a yes! Theresa and KR shot the breeze just like two long-lost souls. Separated for centuries.

Feeling a connection of some sort reminiscent of the past. He finished his shift.

The pocket watch indicated one pm. Two tires to install and balance would take the rest of the day. Procrastinating for a while. Then proceeded to the task at hand. While enjoying some Black Foot played loud. Psycho would be stopping by in the morning for pick up. With the task finished. KR could smell the cabbage rolls cooking. His stomach growled. He dived right in. Rounding out his evening with Nietzsche and some merlot.

Receiving a text before sunrise. Psycho was en route. It would take him at least an hour. Wakening from his slumber. Feeling the cobwebs within. And the lack of sleep. Decided to taper off the Merlot.

Psycho blasted in like a spaceship. One of those big tired trucks. That takes a step ladder to enter. Fell to the ground from the driver's seat. With a grin from ear to ear. Standing five foot six in black leather boots. Cracked a beer and smiled. The sun reflected off his stainless rings. Sat down to bullshit.

Psycho was a little rough around the edges with a heart as big as a bear. And was always there to lend a helping hand when needed. While loading the tires. Slid KR some cabbage mentioning his interest in the California trip. Blasting off he disappeared.

A lingering sense of melancholy was in the air this particular day. KR felt an urge to visit an old friend. He would plan a day trip for Saturday. Leave early and return that evening. Couple hundred miles round trip. Ride hard and fast. Keeping the wind at his back. The pan needed some consecutive hard miles. It would be a good test for the new pressure plate. Sent a text. Return reply the door is open.

Hitting the road early. Just as the sun started to rise. It was beautiful. Reminded him of Theresa. As the crisp air hit his face. The thump of the v twin led the way. Heading north with the wind at his back. KR sped up. The Harley ran well within its power ban between eighty and a hundred. Never grumbling when more was needed.

Entering Beaver Lake County. With the city behind him, a fuel stop was needed. Never going below half a tank was motto number four. Added ten dollars of high octane engaged first. Headed north. Accelerating he noticed red and blue lights up ahead. Roadside stop check. Turning left on a ridge road detoured the check stop. Accessing the highway further north.

LANDING population twenty-five hundred one mile ahead. A sleepy little town built on one side of a gorge. The river Acheron flows through the center. A ferry is the only way to cross. Nobody ever used it. But the ferryman was always on duty. Fuel would be added before the visit.

Wolf was an old-school Ukrainian. Never afraid of hard work. Made his living building log cabins. Harvesting the logs from inherited land. His business thrived. Shipping cabin packages all over the country. He became very prosperous. Never forgetting his roots. Was still a very humble man. Retiring to a life of solitude. Pondered the lunacy of man. Was wise beyond his years.

KR rolled in the drive shutting down the pan. Receiving a bear hug from Wolf. Headed indoors to break some bread. Lunch had been prepared. The table set with Ukrainian favourites. Pickles, sausage. Beet soup, cheese, baked bread. Pickled fish, poppy seed loaf. Washing it all down with a shot of shine. Taking a load off in the den. Listening to the latest Helix release. Sipping on some Earl Gray. Sharing stories from the past. Enjoyed a pull from an oil joint. Sat back and relaxed.

Checked his pocket watch. Four 20 time to roll. Suiting up while the pan warmed. KR exclaimed to Wolf. **DON'T PAY THE FERRYMAN UNTIL HE GETS YOU TO THE OTHER SIDE!** Ready to ride. KR released the clutch and headed south. The visit did him good. The hardtail effortlessly hauled it's passenger home. The frequency of the pan was meditating. Feeling Theresa enter through the backdoor of his mind. Smiling as he shifted into fifth.

TWO
MIDNIGHT

KR ended his day with Nietzsche and a cup of goat weed tea. Reflective of his day. With a sigh swallowed some tea continuing to read. Acknowledging Nietzsche as one of the greatest minds in history. Drifting off to sleep.

As his eyelids flickered open a new day had begun. Destiny had scheduled a midnight rendezvous. Just like you would read in a novel. KR was ecstatic and could not wait. His whole day was spent working on the new build counting the hours. Daydreaming until the hour was near.

The Tower & Crown was not far. Deciding to walk. To could clear his head and relax. Arriving early. He sat at the bar with his back facing the door. He waited. Checked his pocket watch. Twelve sharp! The door swung open he turned. Theresa walked toward him. Throwing her arms around him. It was surreal! `This was life before insanity!` Question answered. His soul had been shaken and stirred by this strange connection. And he wanted more. She was an enigmatic part of his puzzle. But where did she fit in?

HER

A STRAND OF HAIR HUNG TO ONE SIDE OVER HER FACE AT THAT INSTANT I WAS REMINISCENT OF THE PAST DRAWN TO HER FOR ONLY A MOMENT TIME STOOD STILL AND SHE WAS GONE BUT IN MY DREAMS SHE REMAINS HAUNTING ME THROUGHOUT THE DAY ENDING IN SLEEPLESS NIGHTS PASSING SLOWLY UNTIL SUNRISE ALWAYS THERE WHENEVER SHE WANTS IN MY MIND SHE IS THERE WHENEVER SHE WANTS AWAKEN MY MIRROR AWAKEN

~RBK

GLOSSARY

CABBAGE - MONEY
CHOP   - MOTORCYCLE
RIP   - OUT FOR A RIDE
SHINE   - ALCOHOL ILLEGALLY DISTILLED
SPLIFF   - A MARIJUANA CIGARETTE
OIL JOINT- POT OIL MIXED WITH MARIJUANA
FXR   - HARLEY MODEL
HARDTAIL - MOTORCYCLE / NO REAR SUSPENSION
PAN HEAD - DISCONTINUED ENGINE
SHVL   - DISCONTINUED ENGINE
CONE KNUCKLE - CUSTOM ENGINE
CHOPPER   - CUSTOM MOTORCYCLE
RUB   - RICH URBAN BIKER
SUPER G   - HARLEY CARBURATOR
WICK   -HAND THROTTLE

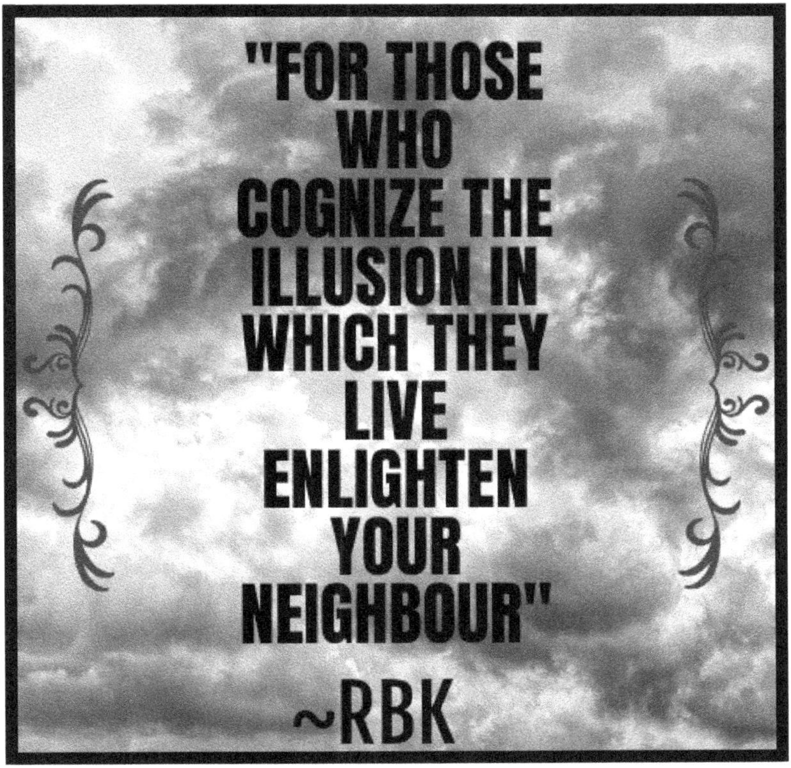

" may your journey be with ease & grace"

PART 1 - THE AWAKENING SOUL SERIES

FOR HER

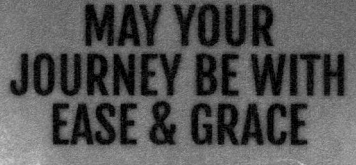

www.ingramcontent.com/pod-product-compliance
Lightning Source LLC
Chambersburg PA
CBHW052114200426
43209CB00076B/1956/J